F. A. Blackmer

Gospel in Song

A new collection of hymns and spiritual songs, for use in Sunday schools,

praise meetings, prayer meetings, revival meetings

F. A. Blackmer

Gospel in Song
A new collection of hymns and spiritual songs, for use in Sunday schools, praise meetings, prayer meetings, revival meetings

ISBN/EAN: 9783337083687

Printed in Europe, USA, Canada, Australia, Japan

Cover: Foto ©Lupo / pixelio.de

More available books at **www.hansebooks.com**

Gospel in Song.

A

NEW COLLECTION

OF

"HYMNS AND SPIRITUAL SONGS."

FOR USE IN

SUNDAY SCHOOLS, PRAISE MEETINGS, PRAYER
MEETINGS, REVIVAL MEETINGS, CAMP
MEETINGS, AND IN OTHER PLACES
WHERE THE NAME OF THE
LORD IS EXALTED
IN SONG.

———◇———

BY

F. A. BLACKMER.

———————

Springfield, Mass.

Published by F. A. BLACKMER.

PREFACE.

— ·· ◇·

It is with great pleasure that we hereby express our deep obligations to those who have enriched the pages of this book by kindly granting the use of their choicest compositions.

We send it forth, hoping and praying that the blessing of the Lord may accompany it, making it prove to the hearts of some who know not the blessed gospel of the Son of God as the title declares: "Gospel in Song"—good news in song; and that it may cheer the path of those who here confess themselves to be pilgrims and strangers, while journeying towards that not far distant home, where the burdens of life are all laid down, and where for "rest no more we sigh."

F. A. BLACKMER.

Do You Know the Wondrous Story?

J. E. HALL.　　　　　　　　　　　　　　　　J. E. HALL.

1. Do　you know the wondrous sto - ry, Have you ev - er heard it told,
2. Have you heard how much He suf-fered. Hanging on the cru - el tree,
3. Is　'it true that you have heard it, Have the tidings reached your ear?

How　that Je - sus came from heav-en, Seek - ing lost ones from the fold?
That　we　all might have sal - va - tion, And might live e - ter - nal - ly?
Then　why not just now be-lieve　it, And find comfort, hope and cheer?

CHORUS.

Do　you know the wondrous sto - ry, Have you ev - er heard it told?

Do　you know the wondrous sto - ry, That with tell-ing ne'er grows old?

By permission.

3

Sweetly Resting.

No. 2.

MARY D. JAMES.

W. WARREN BENTLEY. By per.

1. In the rift - ed Rock I'm resting, Safely sheltered I a - bide;
2. Long pursued by sin and Sa- tan, Weary, sad, I long'd for rest;
3. Peace, which passeth understanding, Joy, the world can never give,
4. In the rift - ed Rock I'll hide me, Till the storms of life are past,

There no foes nor storms molest me, While within the cleft I hide.
Then I found this heav'nly shel - ter, Open'd in my Saviour's breast.
Now in Je - sus I am find - ing; In His smiles of love I live.
All se - cure in this blest ref - uge, Heeding not the fiercest blast.

REFRAIN.

Now I'm rest - ing, sweetly rest - ing, In the cleft once made for me;

Je - sus, bless - ed Rock of A - ges, I will hide myself in Thee.

The Sure Foundation.

"Behold, I lay in Zion for a foundation a stone, a tried stone, a precious corner-stone, a sure foundation."

"For other foundation can no man lay than that is laid, which is Jesus Christ."

No. 3.

F. A. B.   F. A. BLACKMER.

Copyright, 1884, by F. A. Blackmer

1. I will build my house up-on the Rock, And I know it will stand for-ev-er;
2. No foun-da-tion can by man be laid, Than the one which the Lord hath ta-ken;
3. On the sol-id Rock I'll dwell se-cure, And I'll sing of the sure foun-da-tion,

Tho' the rains descend and fierce winds blow, I am sure it will fall, no nev-er.
'Tis a Corner Stone precious, e-lect, By the tempests of earth ne'er sha-ken.
Till the storms of life are o-ver-past, Then rejoice in complete sal-va-tion.

Chorus.

Christ is the Rock, Christ is the Rock, Rock of my sal-va-tion;

Here will I build, here will I build, On the sure foun-da-tion

5

Cast thy Bread upon the Waters.

F. A. BLACKMER.

1. Cast thy bread up-on the wa - ters, Ye who have but scant sup - ply;
2. Cast thy bread up-on the wa - ters, Poor and weary, worn with care,
3. Cast thy bread up-on the wa - ters, Ye who have a - bundant store;
4. Cast thy bread up-on the wa - ters, Far and wide your treasure strew:
5. Cast thy bread up-on the wa - ters, Waft it on with prayerful breath;

An-gel eyes will watch a - bove it, You shall find it bye and bye.
Of-ten sit - ting in the shadows, Have you not a crumb to spare?
It may float on many bil-lows, It may strand on many a shore;
Scatter it with willing fingers; Laugh for joy to see it go;
In some dis - tant, doubtful moment It may save a soul from death:

He who in His righteous balance Doth each hu - man action weigh,
Can you not to those a-round you Sing some lit - tle song of hope,
You may think it lost for - ev - er; But as sure as God is true,
For if you too close-ly keep it, It will on - ly drag you down;
Or when you shall sleep in silence, 'Neath the morn and evening dew,

Will your sac - ri-fice re - mem-ber, Will your loving deed re - pay.
While you look with longing vis - ion Thro' faith's mighty tel-es - cope?
In this life or in the oth - er, It will yet re-turn to you.
If you love it more than Je - sus, It will keep you from your crown.
Stranger hands that you have strengthen'd May strew lilies o - ver you.

6

CHORUS.

Cast thy bread . . . Cast thy bread

Cast thy bread upon the waters, Cast thy bread upon the waters;

Cast thy bread On His word,

Cast thy bread upon the waters, On His word ye can rely, ye can rely;

Angel eyes

Angel eyes will watch above it, You shall find it bye and bye.

No. 5. ## The Sinners' Friend.

1. O Thou, the con-trite sin-ners' friend! Who, loving, lov'st them to the end,
2. When weary in the Christian race, Far off appears my resting place,
3. When I have err'd and gone a - stray, Afar from Thine and wisdom's way,
4. When Satan, by my sins made bold, Strives from Thy cross to loose my hold,
5. And when my dy - ing hour draws near, Darken'd with anguish, guilt, and fear,
6. When the full light of heav'n-ly day Reveals my sins in dread ar - ray,

On this a-lone my hopes de-pend, That Thou wilt plead for me.
And, faint - ing, I mistrust Thy grace, Then, Savior, plead for me.
And see no glimmering, guiding ray, Still, Savior, plead for me.
Then with Thy pity-ing arms en - fold, And plead, oh, plead for me.
Then to my fainting sight ap-pear, Pleading in heav'n for me.
Say Thou hast wash'd them all a - way; Oh, say Thou plead'st for me.

Beautiful City of God.

No. 6.

F. A. B.

F. A. BLACKMER.

1. Oh, beau-ti-ful ci - ty, Oh, glo - ri - ous ci - ty, Fore-seen by the seer in his
2. Oh, won - derful ci - ty, oh, heaven-built ci - ty, Je - ru - salem golden, blest
3. Oh, beau-ti-ful ci - ty, oh, long-looked-for ci - ty, By patriarchs, prophets and
4. There sin can - not harm, for to all that's un - ho - ly Those pearly gates never an
5. Oh, jew - el-decked ci - ty, oh, bright, shining ci - ty, Blest ci - ty of God, we are

vis - ion so bright, De - scending in grandeur from God out of heav - en, And
ci - ty of light; Where Je - sus shall reign, and His wonderful presence Shall
worth - ies of old; We watch for thy coming as they watched before us, And
en - trance can give; All pass - ing those portals are ransomed immor-tals; For-
pin - ing for thee; Oh, soon may we rest in thy mansions of glo - ry, Where

CHORUS.

shin - ing in garments of pure jas-per light. Beau - ti ful ci - ty,
ban - ish for - ev - er the darkness of night.
sigh for thy beauties and pleasures un-told.
ev - er in glo - ry with Je - sus they live.
we shall for - ev - er from sorrow be free.

Beautiful, beautiful ci - ty of God,

Beau - ti-ful ci-ty of God, Oh, when .... shall I roam thro' thy
Beau-ti-ful, beau-ti-ful, Oh, when shall I roam thro' thy streets of pure gold, Thro' thy

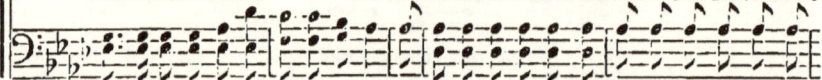

streets of pure gold? Beau - ti-ful ci - ty, Beau - ti-ful ci-ty of God,
wonderful streets, Beautiful, beautiful ci-ty of God, Beautiful, beautiful

8

Beautiful City of God.—CONCLUDED.

Thy glo - - - ry re-splen - dent I long.......... to be - hold.
Thy glo - ry resplendent, thy glo - ry resplendent I long, oh, I long

Come, Drink of the Water.

"Whosoever drinketh of this water shall thirst again; but whosoever drinketh
of the water that I shall give him shall never thirst."—John iv: 13, 14.

No. 7.

A. F.   A. FRANCIS.

1. Oh, wondrous words that Je - sus spake To thirst-y souls, a sweet re-frain;
2. Won - drous the words, more wondrous still That promise doth for us re-main,
3. Ye souls a - thirst for life and peace, Let not this message come in vain;

"Who drinks the draught that I shall give, Shall . nev - er thirst a - gain."
And we may of the wa - ter drink, And nev - er thirst a - gain.
But quick - ly take the cleansing draught, And nev - er thirst a - gain.

CHORUS.

Come, drink of the wa - ter; come, drink of the water of life; Who drinks of the water that

Christ shall give Shall nevermore thirst, but evermore live; Come, drink of the water of life.

Copyright, 1884, by F. A. Packever.

9

What Must it be to be There.

No. 8.

"For now we see through a glass, darkly; but then face to face."—1 Cor. xiii. 12.

MRS. ELIZABETH MILLS.　　　　　　　　　　　F. A. BLACKMER.

1. We speak of the land of the   blest, A   country so bright and so   fair :
2. We speak of its pathways of gold, Its walls decked with jewels so rare;
3. We speak of the peace it shall bring, The robes that the ransomed shall wear,
4. We speak of its freeedom from sin, From   sorrow, temptation and care,
5. That country we soon shall be - hold, Its   glo - ry increasing shall share;

And   oft are its glories con - fest;　But what must it be   to be   there.
Its   wonders and pleasures untold;　But what must it be   to be   there.
The songs of rejoicing they'll sing;　But what must it be   to be   there.
From   trials without and within;　But what must it be   to be there.
Then we   as its pleasures unfold.　Shall know what it is   to be   there.

CHORUS.

Oh, what must it be to be there.　　Oh, what must it be to   be there,
　　　　　　　　to be there,　　　　　　　　　　　　　　to be there;

We   of - ten the glory con - fess; But what must it be   to be   there.

Never Alone.

No. 9.

R. W. RAYMOND.   FERD. SILCHER.

1. Far out on the des-o-late bil - low, The sail - or   sails the   sea,
2. Far down in the earth's dark bosom, The min - er   mines the   ore;
3. Forth in-to the dread-ful bat - tle The steadfast   sol - dier   goes,
4. Lord, grant as we sail life's o - cean, Or delve in   its mines of woe;

Alone with the night and the tempest, Where countless dan-gers   be!
Death lurks in the dark behind   him, And hides in the rock be - fore.
No friend when he lies a   dy - ing, His eyes to   kiss and   close.
Or fight in its ter-ri-ble con - flict, This com-fort all   to   know.

CHORUS.

Yet,
Yet,
Yet. } nev - er a - lone is the Christian, Who lives by faith and prayer;
That,

For God   is a Friend un - fail - ing, And God   is   eve - ry - where.

11

The Grand Review.

" And before Him shall be gathered all nations."— Matt. xxv: 32.

F. A. B.

F. A. BLACKMER.

1. Christian soldier worn with service, Ere discharge is granted you,
2. Gird your armor on tho' rust-ed, Soon with use 'twill shine a-new;
3. If you do each du-ty brave-ly, Then the Lord will hon-or you;
4. There'll be glory for the he-roes, Who for God shall here be true,

You must pass Di-vine in-spec-tion At the fi-nal grand re-view.
And in Heaven's strength go for-ward, Ready for the grand re-view.
And your val-or He'll re-mem-ber At the fi-nal grand re-view.
When they're mustered out of service, And have passed the grand re-view.

CHORUS.

Oh, be watch - ful Christian sol - dier, At your
watchful Christian sol-dier, Oh, be watchful Christian soldier, At your

post .... stand firm and true;......... At your
post stand firm and true, stand firm and true;... ... Read-y
At your post stand firm and true;

post,............

for............ the great in-spec - tion,
for . the great in-spec - tion, Read-y for the great inspection, Ready

12

for.................... the grand re - view......

for the grand re - view,

There is Pardon for you

No. 11.

A. F.

A. FRANCIS.

1. O, come to the Saviour, to-day He invites, That Sav-iour so good and so true,
2. O, come to the Saviour, poor wanderer, come; You would not resist if you knew
3. O, come to the Saviour, come, bidding the world With all its allurements a - dieu!
4. O, come to the Saviour and pray that He will Your heart by His Spirit re - new;

Who loves you while yet you are going astray, And of - fers full pardon to you.
How much He has suffered that He might redeem, And grant a full pardon to you.
O, come and find welcome, and comfort, and home; O haste! while there's pardon for you.
There's danger in waiting, O, seek Him to-day, For now there is pardon for you.

CHORUS...

O yes, there is pardon for you,.... O yes, there is pardon for you;....
O yes, there is pardon,   is pardon for you;

For Je-sus is a - ble and willing to save; O yes, there is par-don for you.

No dying there.

No. 12.

F. A. B.   F. A. BLACKMER.

"And God shall wipe away all tears from their eyes; and there shall be no more death." Rev. xxi: 4.

1. A land by faith I see, Where saints shall ev - er be
2. There friends shall meet a - gain, In hap - pi - ness to reign;
3. There sor - row can - not stay; There tears are wiped a - way;
4. O, land of beau - ty rare, Free from earth-blight and care,

Free from mor - tal - i - ty, No dying there.
While thro' that blest do - main, No dying there.
One bright, e - ter - nal day, No dying there.
Thy bliss I long to share. No dying there.

No dy - ing there,.......... No dy - ing there;..........

CHORUS.

No dy-ing there,   No dy - ing there;

rit.

In that fair, heav'nly land, No dying there, no dy - ing there.

5 For such a priceless boon,
  Who would not seek that home?
  Safe from the dreaded tomb,
  No dying there.

6 For thee, sweet home, I wait;
  Come, and my soul elate;
  Welcome, O deathless state,
  No dying there.

14

Keep Me, Lord.

No. 13.

I. I. L.   I. I. LESLIE.

1. Keep me, Lord, from wandering from Thee; Guide my feet from ev - 'ry tempting snare;
2. Thro' the darkness as I hast-en on, Be Thou near to guard me in the way:
3. Where Thou art there can be nought to fear: From Thy presence harm and dangers flee;
4. Onward, then, my feet, along the way He has gone, the Saviour of my soul,

Where I go, where-ev-er I may be, Let Thy gra - cious, keeping hand be there.
Till the night and shadows all are gone, Saviour, Mas - ter, deign with me to stay.
Foes may rise and en - e-mies be near, They are safe who close-ly fol - low Thee.
Till I reach the bright and perfect day, And my bro - ken spir - it is made whole.

CHORUS.

All the way I here may go, All the way I may not know;

Ev-er near my Guide and Guardian be, 'Till the Ci - ty's shining gates I see.

15

The Rescue.

G. W. S.   G. W. SEDERQUIST.

1. Man - y souls on life's dark   ocean, Without helm, or sail, or oar,
2. See   the lighthouse watcher, keeping Eve - ry bea-con shining bright;
3. Hold the light for one   an - oth-er: "Tis thy loving Lord's command;
4. Lift   the light up high - er, higher! Thousands, thousands need your aid;

Struggling with the waves' com-mo-tion, Seek   a qui - et rest on shore.
Wak - ing while the world is   sleep-ing: Wrapt in thick-est shades of night.
Seize the ship-wrecked drowning brother With   a man - ly lov-ing hand.
Throw its flash - es nigh - er,   nigh - er; Plead and urge, constrain, persuade.

Christ-ian brother, join   to   la - bor, By the light of love di - vine;
There is many an o - cean ran - ger Tost up - on   the dreadful shoals;
Rouse him up to life and ac-tion; Quick apply   the means to save;
Bor - row torch-es from the al - tar, Blaz-ing like the noon-day sun.

Help   to save thy drowning neighbor; Trim thy lamp and let it shine.
Friends and comrades are in   dan-ger, Haste to save their precious souls.
And   by love's di - vine at - trac-tion, Lift him, lift him from the wave.
Hold   them up, nor flag, nor falter, Till thou hear the words, "Well done."

CHORUS.

Haste! to the rescue, Fear not wind or wave; God's grace will aid you Sinking ones to save.

Walk in the Marvelous Light.

"Out of darkness into His marvelous light."

F. A. BLACKMER.

1. Walk in the light! and thou shalt know.... The fel-low-ship of love,
2. Walk in the light! and thou shalt own..... Thy darkness passed a - way,
3. Walk in the light! and e'en the tomb...... No fearful shade shall wear;
4. Walk in the light! thy path shall be...... Peace-ful, serene and bright;

His Spir - it on - ly can be - stow, ... Who reigns in light a - bove.
Be - cause that light hath on thee shone..... In which is per-fect day.
Glo - ry shall chase away the gloom, ... For Christ hath conquer'd there.
For God, by grace, shall dwell in thee, ... And God himself is light.

CHORUS.

Walk.... in the light,.... Walk .. in the light,
Walk in the light, the mar-vel-ous light, Walk in the light, the mar-vel-ous light,

Walk...... in the light,......
The marvelous light, the light of God, Walk in the light, the mar-vel-ous light,

Walk.... in the light,
Walk in the light, the marvelous light, Oh, walk in the marvelous light of God.

17

Oh! while the Moments Linger.

F. A. B.   F. A. BLACKMER.

1. Oh! while the moments linger, There's work for us to do;
2. Oh! plead not vain ex - cus- es, There's work for eve - ry one;
3. Oh! let us do each du - ty, As God shall make it plain;
4. Our work will soon be end- ed, Our tri - als soon be o'er;

The Mas - ter bids us la - bor, And in His cause be true.
There are kind words to be spoken, And kind deeds to be done.
If He shall bless our la - bor, It can - not be in vain.
And then we'll rest in glo - ry With Je - sus ev - er - more.

CHORUS.

Oh! while the moments lin - ger, Oh! while the moments lin - ger

There's work to do, There's work to do, There's work for us to do.

He Calleth Thee.

G. W. S.

G. W. SEDERQUIST.

1. The Saviour is coming; He calleth for thee; Awake and the message receive;
2. The Saviour is coming; He calleth thee now; Olf! enter His vineyard to day;
3. The Saviour is coming; a crown He will give To all who are faithful and tried;
4. The Saviour will call from the heavens above; The angels obey His command,

His blood is the ransom, thy pardon is free, If thou wilt repent and believe.
To labor and toil, with the sweat on thy brow, And whate'er is right He will pay.
The just and the pure shall e-ter-nal-ly live, In Zi - on for-ev - er a-bide.
And gath-er His saints to the E - den of love, To dwell in that beautiful land.

CHORUS.

Earnestly la-bor, pa-tient-ly la - bor; Labor for Je-sus till He shall come,

rit.

Earn - est-ly la - bor, pa-tient-ly la- bor, Till He appears and welcomes you home.

19

Beautiful World of Light.

(DUETT AND CHORUS.)

No. 18.

A. T. G.

A. T. GORHAM.
By permission.

1. A few more days to brave the blast, The surging tide to stem,
2. A few more bit-ter tears to shed, Where sorrows o - ver-flow;
3. Take courage, sailors, for the night Is nearing un - to day;

And we shall gain our ha-ven home, And wear Life's di - a-dem.
A few more wan-ing days to thread The paths of want and woe;
The bow of hope shall span the cloud, As earth-mists roll a - way.

Be - yond the curl - ing waves I see The hills of glo - ry bright;
Be val-iant, tho' the bil-lows foam, The life-boat is in sight;
Take courage, for the dawn shall break In gold-en glo - ry bright;

SEMI-CHORUS.

cres.

Will you be there? Yes, we'll be there, In that beautiful world of light.

20

Beautiful World of Light.—CONCLUDED.

CHORUS.

Soon we shall roam the morning fields, Be - yond the shores of night;

cres.

Will you be there? Yes, we'll be there! In that beautiful world of light.

rit.

That beautiful, beautiful, beautiful world, That beautiful world of light.

Newcomb. L. M.

No. 19.

F. A. BLACKMER.

1. Stay, thou in-sult - ed Spir-it, stay, Tho' I have done thee such de - spite;
2. Though I have most un-faith-ful been Of all who e'er thy grace re - ceived,
3. Yet, Oh, the chief of sinners spare, In hon-or of my great High Priest;
4. My wea-ry soul, O God, release; Uphold me with thy gracious hand;

Cast not a sin-ner quite a-way, Nor take thine ev - er - last - ing flight.
Ten thousand times thy goodness seen, Ten thousand times thy goodness grieved;
Nor, in thy righteous anger, swear I shall not see thy peo - ple's rest.
Oh, guide me in - to perfect peace, And bring me to the promised land.

He that goeth forth and weepeth.

No. 20.

J. E. H. By permission. J. E. HALL.

DUET. SOP, OR ALTO.

1. He that go - eth forth and weepeth, Bear - ing precious seed,
2. He that go - eth forth and weepeth, Trust - ing in the Lord,
3. He that go - eth forth and weepeth, All a - glow with love,
4. He that go - eth forth and weepeth, Christ he nev - er leaves,

TENOR.

Let him know that as he soweth To the sinner's need, So he'll reap.
Let him know that all he soweth Of the precious word, That he'll reap.
Oft-en-times, just while he soweth, Hearts begin to move; So he'll reap.
Doubtless shall return rejoicing! Bringing home his sheaves, Thus, he'll reap.

CHORUS. p f

p

Sowing now, sowing now, But reaping by and by:
Sowing now, sowing now,

p p f

Weeping now, weeping now, Re - joic - ing by and by.
Weeping now, weeping now,

The Love of Christ.

No. 21.

"The love of Christ which passeth knowledge." —Eph. iii. 19.

F. A. B.

F. A. BLACKMER.

1. The love of Christ is boundless, It reach-eth e - ven me;
2. The love of Christ is constant, Whate'er doth me be - tide
3. The love of Christ, how precious! What can I want be - side,

The mys - tic tie is stron-ger Than hu-man love can be!
His bless - ed presence cheers me, He walketh by my side;
Since all things they in - her - it Who in that love a - bide?

Beyond a friend or broth-er, He lov - eth as no oth - er;
Af - fec - tion nev - er ceas - ing, My soul's de - sire ap-peas - ing;
On earth how sweet the sto - ry, 'Twill sweeter be in glo - ry;

CHORUS.

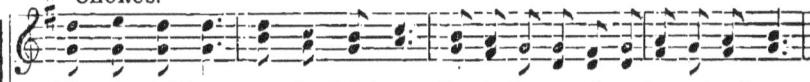

Won-der-ful love, won-der-ful love. Carol it mortals, and angels a-bove;

Won-der-ful love, won-der-ful love, Won-der-ful love of Je - sus.

23

Look to Jesus.

JOSEPHINE POLLARD.   C. E. POLLOCK.

1. Look to Je-sus, wea-ry one, Full of an-guish, full of grief;
2. See! the lov-ing Saviour stands, Pleading for thy fond em-brace;
3. Look to Je-sus; not in vain Do the wea-ry seek for rest:

He will comfort, He a-lone Has the balm for thy re-lief;
Trust thyself to Je-sus' hands, In His bo-som hide thy face:
Weep a-way thy tears and pain, Like a child up-on His breast.

Look to Him in thy de-spair, Rest and ref-uge He will give,
All thy sick-ness He can cure, All thy sins He will for-give,
Breathe thy sorrow in His ear, Strength for ev-'ry day re-ceive;

rit.....................

All thy bur-dens He will bear, Look to Je-sus, look and live.
He will make His promise sure, Look to Je-sus, look and live.
Light in dark-ness will ap-pear, If thou wilt but look and live.

From " Welcome Songs," by permission F. H. Revell.

Beautiful Zion.

No. 23.

F. A. BLACKMER.

Copyright, 1884, by F. A. Blackmer.

1. Beau-ti - ful Zi - on, built a - bove, Beau - ti - ful
Beau - ti - ful Zi - on,

ci - ty that I love, Beau - ti - ful gates
Beau - ti - ful ci - ty Beau - ti - ful

of pearly white, Beau-ti-ful tem - ple— God its light;
gates of Beautiful temple—

He, who was slain on Cal - va-ry, O - pens those pearly gates to me.

2 Beautiful city fill'd with light,
Beautiful angels, clothed in white,
Beautiful strains that never tire,
Beautiful harps thro' all the choir;
There shall I join the chorus sweet,
Worshiping at the Savior's feet.

3 Beautiful crowns on every brow,
Beautiful palms the conquerors show,
Beautiful robes the ransomed wear,

Beautiful all who enter there;
Thither I press with eager feet,
There shall my rest be long and sweet.

4 Beautiful throne of Christ, our King,
Beautiful songs the angels sing,
Beautiful rest, all wanderings cease,
Beautiful home of perfect peace;
There shall my eyes the Savior see,—
Haste to this heavenly home with me.

Sowing and Reaping.

They that sow in tears shall reap in joy.—Ps. cxxvi. 5.

JOSEPHINE POLLARD.　　　　　　　　　　　　EDWARD A. PERKINS.

Thoughtfully.

1. Out on the highways, wherev-er we go, Seed we must gather and seed we must sow;
2. Out of those gardens so gorgeous with flow'rs, Seed we may gather to beau-ti-fy ours;

E - ven the tin - i - est seed has a power, Be it of this-tle or be it a flower.
While from our own little plot we may share Something to render our neighbor's more fair.

a tempo.

Here, where it seems but a wilderness place, Wanting in beauty and wanting in grace,
Out of each moment some good we obtain, Something to winnow and scat-ter a-gain;

Some lit-tle creature in tenderness goes, Plucking the nettle and planting the rose.
All that we lis-ten to, all that we read, All that we think of is gath - er-ing seed.

CHORUS.

Gath - er-ing seed........ we must scat - ter as
That........ which we gath - er is that .... which we

Gath - er - ing seed we must scat - ter as well, Gath - er - ing seed we must
That which we gather is that which we sow, That which we gath - er is

From "Welcome Songs," by permission F. H. Revell.

Sowing and Reaping. CONCLUDED.

well.......... God........ will watch o - - ver the
sow... .... Seed time and har - - vest al-

scat - ter as well; God will watch o - ver the place where it fell,
that which we sow, Seed - time and harvest al - ter - nate - ly flow,

place...... where it fell........ On - ly the gain.... of the
ter - nate - ly flow ...... When we have fin - ished with

God will watch over the place where it fell,
Seedtime and harvest al - ter - nate - ly flow,

har - vest is ours— Shall we plant nettles, or shall we plant flowers?
time, 't will be known How we have gathered, and how we have sown.

Leslie.

No. 25.

F. A. BLACKMER.

1. Come un - to me when shadows darkly gather, When the sad heart is weary and distress'd.
2. Ye who have mourn'd when the spring flow'rs were taken, When the ripe fruit fell richly to the ground.
3. There, like an Eden blossoming in gladness, Shall bloom those flowers the earth too rudely pressed.

Seeking for comfort from your heav'nly Father. Come un-to me, and I will give you rest.
When lov'd ones slept, in brighter homes to waken, When they with life eternal shall be crown'd.
"Come unto me," all ye who droop in sadness, "Come unto me, and I will give you rest!"

27

Love and Grace.

No. 26.

I. L. L.

I. L. LESLIE.

1. Oh! 'twas love that brought me to Him, And 'tis love that keeps me there;
2. Dark it was be - fore I found Him, And the way I could not see;
3. Oh, how blest to walk with Je - sus! Joy we nev - er knew be - fore;
4. Now it is by faith I view Him, As I walk this narrow way;
5. Then my joy will be for - ev - er; There no clouds will in - ter - vene;

By His grace it was I knew Him, Now my Sav - ior dear and fair.
Now the light that shines around Him, As I fol - low, falls on me.
From our fears His presence frees us, While we trust Him more and more.
But He soon will call me to Him, In that bright approaching day.
And the dark - ness comes there never— I shall see Him as I'm seen.

CHORUS.

Love and grace, His love and grace, I will sing in ev - 'ry place,

Till I reach that blissful shore, Where I'll praise Him ever - more!

Copyright, 1884, by F. A. Blackmer.

28

Just as I Am.

No. 27.

MISS CHARLOTTE ELLIOT.   F. A. BLACKMER.

1. Just as I am, without one plea, But that Thy blood was shed for me,
2. Just as I am, and waiting not To rid my soul of one dark blot,
3. Just as I am, tho' tossed about With many a conflict, many a doubt,
4. Just as I am, poor, wretched, blind; Sight, riches, healing of the mind,
5. Just as I am, Thou wilt receive, Wilt welcome, pardon, cleanse, relieve;
6. Just as I am, Thy love unknown Has broken every barrier down :

And that Thou bid'st me come to thee, O Lamb of God! I come, I   come!
To thee, whose blood can cleanse each spot, O Lamb of God! I come, I   come!
Fightings within, and fears with-out, O Lamb of God! I come, I   come!
Yea, all I need in Thee to find, O Lamb of God! I come, I   come!
Because thy promise I be-lieve, O Lamb of God! I come, I   come!
Now to be Thine, yea, Thine a-lone, O Lamb of God! I come, I   come!

CHORUS.

With all my guilt,   I come to Thee,   O let Thy
With all my guilt,   I come to Thee,

blood .... a - tone for me; ....   For - ever -
O   let   thy blood   a-tone for me;

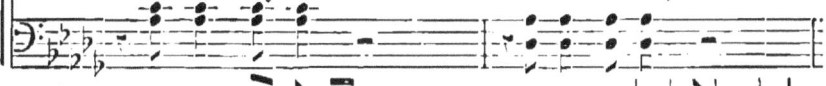

more .... Thine own to be, ... O Lamb of God! I come!
Forev - er more   Thine own to be,

29

We'll Live in Tents.

No. 28.

Heb. xi. 8—13.

G. H. S.　　　　　　　　　　　　　　　　　　　　　　G H. S.

1. God bids His people on the earth, Ere yet He comes and calls them hence,
2. It　　is His will that we should pass Like strangers, sep-a-rate, a - side,
3. He'd have us rear　　no stately towers, Sink no foundation walls of stone,
4. O　　broth-er, what - so - ev-er chain Binds us to flesh - ly lust and strife,

To live un-knit　to home and hearth, Like far-bound travelers— in tents.
From all the world-enamored mass That crowd the Bab-y-lons　of pride.
But camp each night a few short hours, And ere the morrow's dawn move on.
Here let us rend　it in God's name, And live, henceforth, the pilgrim life.

CHORUS.

We'll live in tents　un-til our feet　Shall reach the land　by sin untrod,

We'll live in tents　until our feet　shall reach the land

The gate of pearl, the gold-en　street, Whose builder and whose maker, God.

From "Welcome Songs," by permission F. H. Revell.

Oh, 'Tis Wonderful!

I. I. LESLIE. F A. BLACKMER.

1. When I was far a-way and lost, Oh, 'tis won-der-full That I was saved at such a cost! Oh, 'tis won-der-full

CHORUS.

Oh, 'tis won-der-full Oh,... 'tis won-der-ful, That Je-sus gave His life for me! Oh, 'tis won-der-ful!

2 I once was blind, but now I see;
Oh, 'tis wonderful!
Was bound by sin, but now am free;
Oh, 'tis wonderful!

3 My guilt was all I had to bring;
Oh, 'tis wonderful!
Yet I was made His love to sing;
Oh, 'tis wonderful!

4 This great salvation all may share;
Oh, 'tis wonderful!
Thro'out the world the message bear;
Oh, 'tis wonderful!

5 Come, sinner, now, and seek His grace;
Oh, 'tis wonderful!
And find in Him a resting place;
Oh, 'tis wonderful!

31

I'm Resting in the Crucified.

No. 30.

"Ye shall find rest unto your souls."—Matt ii. 29.

F A. B.   F. A. BLACKMER.

1. The Cru - ci - fied of Calva - ry Has ta - ken all my load of sin,
2. Wea - ry and sad I Wandered long, Oppressed with burdens hard to bear;
3. Oh, what a resting place is this, And ref - uge for the weary soul,
4. Se - cure from ev'- ry foe am I While rest - ing in the Cruci - fied;

Has cleansed my heart from every stain, And brought the glorious fullness in.
But when the Cru - ci - fied I sought, I found sweet rest and sol - ace there.
Where sin's wild ocean cannot drown, Tho' near its threat'ning billows roll !
Here is a calm and safe re - treat, And here I ev - er would a - bide.

CHORUS.

The Cru - ci - fied of Cal - va - ry, I'm sweetly resting in the Cru - cified;

He saves me now, and all the time, I'm sweetly resting in the Crucified.

Trusting in Thee.

No 31.

A. T. G.

A. T. GORHAM.
By permission.

1. Lord and Redeem - er, list to my cry; Foes now assail me, danger is nigh;
2. Storm-clouds enshroud me, waves overwhelm; Weakly my frail grasp slips from the helm;
3. Safe to Thy haven grant that I come, Goal of my voy - age, refuge and home.

Un - to Thy shelt'ring arms I would flee, Fearing no e - vil, trusting in Thee.
Guide Thou my lone bark over the sea— Keep and defend me, trusting in Thee.
Glorious indeed the triumph shall be— Vict'ry o'er death through trusting in Thee.

REFRAIN.

Trusting in Thee, Lord, trusting in Thee; Thou my high tow'r and covert shall be:

Dark tho' my way, the light I can see, Blessed Redeem - er, trusting in Thee.

33

"The New Song."

No. 32.

H. POLLARD.

SOUTHERN MELODY.

Cho. Wait a lit-tle while, Then we'll sing the New Song;

Wait a lit-tle while, Then we'll sing the New Song.

1. When the great Ju-bi-lee shall come, Then we'll sing the New Song;

End with Chorus.

And Christ shall take his ransom'd home, Then we'll sing the New Song.

2 When the long night of sin shall close,
   Then we'll sing the New Song;
And life's fair day shall end our woes,
   Then we'll sing the New Song.
Cho.—Wait a little while, etc.

3 When the glad shout shall rend the sky,
   Then we'll sing, etc.
"O grave, where is thy victory?"
   Then we'll sing, etc.
Cho.—Wait a little while, etc.

4 When sorrow, pain and death are o'er,
   Then we'll sing, etc.
And sighs and tears shall be no more,
   Then we'll sing, etc.
Cho.—Wait a little while, etc.

5 When to the pearly gates we come,
   Then we'll sing, etc.
When we have reached our blissful home,
   Then we'll sing, etc.
Cho.—Wait a little while, etc.

6 When we shall tread Life's river brink,
   Then we'll sing, etc.
And of those crystal waters drink,
   Then we'll sing, etc.
Cho.—Wait a little while, etc.

7 Where all will be immortal, fair,
   There we'll sing the New Song;
When blood-washed robes are ours to wear,
   Then we'll sing the New Song.
Cho.—Wait a little while, etc.

Why not be Saved To-night?

F. A. BLACKMER.

1. Oh, do not let the word depart, And close thine eyes against the light;
2. To-morrow's sun may never rise To bless thy long de-lu-ded sight;
3. Our God in pi - ty lingers still; And wilt thou thus his love requite?
4. The world has nothing left to give; It has no new, no pure de - light;

Poor sinner, harden not thy heart; Thou would'st be saved, why not to-night?
This is the time; oh, then be wise! Thou would'st be saved, why not to-night?
Renounce at once thy stubborn will; Thou would'st be saved, why not to-night?
Oh, try the life which Christians live; Thou would'st be saved, why not to-night?

CHORUS.

Why not be saved to - night?...... Why not be saved to-night?
Why not be saved to-night? Why not be saved to-night?

Poor sinner, harden not thy heart; Thou would'st be saved, why not to-night?

Blessed Promise.

"Unto them that look for Him shall He appear the second time wthout sin unto salvation."
Heb. 9: 23.

F. A. B.
F. A. BLACKMER.

1. Oh, the promise, blessed promise, How it cheers the pilgrim here;
2. Signs foretold by Christ we've witness'd, On the earth and in the sky;
3. He will bring our long-lost lov'd ones, Cruel death has torn a - way;
4. Glo - ri - ous, in - deed, the prospect, For the King will surely come;

That our Lord, to bring deliv'rance, Will a - gain to men ap - pear.
And we lift our heads rejoic - ing, For re - demp - tion draweth nigh.
We shall greet them at the dawning Of the bright e - ter - nal day.
We shall see Him in His beauty; He will take His peo - ple home.

CHORUS.

Tell a - broad the joy-ful sto - - ry, Till the

Tell a-broad the joyful sto - ry, Tell abroad the joyful story, Till the

dis - - tant nations hear That the Lord of life and

distant nations hear, Till the distant nations hear That the Lord of life and glory, That the

glo - ry Will a - gain to men ap - pear.

Lord of life and glory Will again to men appear,

The Pearl for Me.

F. A. BLACKMER.

1. The pearl that worldlings covet, Is not the pearl for me; Its beau-ty fades as quickly
2. The crown that decks the monarch Is not the crown for me; It daz-zles but a moment,
3. The road that many travel Is not the road for me; It leads to death and sorrow,
4. The hope that sinners cherish Is not the hope for me; Most sure-ly will they perish,

As sunshine on the sea. But there's a pearl sought by the wise; 'Tis called the pearl of
Its brightness soon will flee. But there's a crown prepared above For all who walk in
In it I would not be. But there's a path that leads to God, 'Tis marked by Christ's most
Unless from sin made free. But there's a hope which rests in God, And leads the soul to

greatest price. Tho' few its val-ue see; Oh, that's the pearl for me,
humble love; For-ev-er bright 'twill be; Oh, that's the crown for me,
precious blood. The way for all is free, Oh, that's the path for me,
trust his word And sin-ful pleasures flee; Oh, that's the hope for me,

Oh, that's the pearl for me, Oh, that's the pearl for me,
Oh, that's the crown for me, etc.
Oh, that's the path for me, etc.
Oh, that's the hope for me, etc.
for me, for me.

Yes there's a pearl sought by the wise; Oh, that's the pearl for me.

37

Jehovah's Promise.

MARY A. BAKER.

H. R. PALMER.
By permission.

Exodus. 6. 1—8.

1. Chain'd by sin in cru-el bondage, Groaning with our bitter need,
2. Oh, the wondrous, wondrous mercy, When Je-ho-vah, Lord of all,
3. Oh, the blessed, blessed promise; Not one tittle e'er shall fail,

Drooping 'neath our guilty bur - den, Lord, Thy promises we plead.
Bending from the glorious heav - en, An-swer-eth our feeble call.
Tho' the earth should burn to ashes, And the suns and stars grow pale.

CHORUS.

I, Je - ho - vah, will redeem you, For my name and covenant's sake,

From your burdens I'll release you, All your fetters I will break,

38

And I will take you for a peo-ple; Your Redeemer I will be,

And with an outstretch'd arm I'll rescue Ev'ry soul that trusts in me.

Bear the Cross To-day.

No. 37.

"I will pay my vows unto the Lord now in the presence of all His people." Ps. 116: 14.

F. A. B.   F. A. BLACKMER.

1. Bear the cross for Jesus, Bear the cross to-day;   In His peoples' presence
2. Bear the cross for Jesus, Bear the cross to-day;   Answer when He bids thee,
3. Lis - ten to the Spir-it, Teaching all His will; If thou heed its whisp'rings

CHORUS.

Deign thy vows to   pay.
Speak, or sing, or   pray.   Bear the cross, bear the cross, Bear the cross for
Joy   thy soul shall fill.

Ja - sus; Bear the cross, bear the cross, Bear the cross to - day.

Cross of Christ.

D. T. TAYLOR. By per.

J. C. STODDARD.

1. Cross of Christ, O sa - cred tree, Hide my sins, and shel - ter me;
2. Cross of Christ, O sa - cred tree, Let me to thy shad - ow flee;
3. Cross of Christ, O sa - cred tree, Type of love's deep mys - te - ry;
4. Cross of Christ, O sa - cred tree, This my boast shall ev - er be;

Claim or mer - it have I none, I am vile, and all undone;
Here they mock'd the cru - ci - fied, Here the roy - al suffer - er died:
'Twas my sins provok'd this love, I this matchless pas-sion mov'd;
That the blood for me was shed, That for me He groan'd and bled;

I to thee for suc - cor fly; Give me ref - uge, or I die.
Here was shed th' a-ton - ing blood, Till it crimson'd all the sod.
For my soul this love was stor'd, On my head the bless-ing pour'd.
Now I catch that gra - cious eye, Now I know I shall not die.

Cross of Christ, O sa - cred tree, All my hopes are hung on thee.
Cross of Christ, O sa - cred tree, Can the guilt - y trust in thee?
Cross of Christ, O sa - cred tree, Now I solve love's mys - te - ry.
Cross of Christ, O sa - cred tree, All my guilt is lost in thee.

CHORUS. Cross..... of Christ,.... sa - cred tree;......

sa - cred, sa - cred tree;
Cross of Christ, Cross of Christ, Cross of Christ, O sa - cred tree;

Cross of Christ. CONCLUDED.

Cross of Christ, O sa-cred tree, All my hopes are hung on thee.

Thy Coming Again.

No. 39.

F. A. BLACKMER.

1. I'm wait-ing for Thee, Lord, Thy beauty to see, Lord, I'm waiting for Thee,
2. 'Mid danger and fear, Lord, I'm oft weary here, Lord, The day must be near
3. While Thou art away, Lord, I stumble and stray, Lord, Oh, hasten the day
4. Our loved ones be-fore, Lord, Their troubles are o'er, Lord, I'll meet them once more
5. E'en now let my ways, Lord, Be bright in Thy praise, Lord, For brief are the days

For Thy coming again; Thou'rt gone over there, Lord, A place to prepare, Lord,
Of Thy coming again; 'Tis all sunshine there, Lord, No sigh-ing nor care, Lord,
Of Thy coming again; This is not my rest, Lord, A pil-grim confess'd, Lord,
At Thy coming again; Thy blood was the sign, Lord, That mark'd them as thine, Lord,
Ere Thy coming again; I'm waiting for Thee, Lord, Thy beau-ty to see, Lord,

Thy home I shall share, At Thy com-ing a - gain.
But glo - ry so fair, At Thy com-ing a - gain.
I wait to be blest, At Thy com-ing a - gain.
And bright - ly they'll shine At Thy com-ing a - gain.
No tri - umph for me Like Thy com-ing a - gain.

41

I am the Door.

"I am the door; by Me if any man enter in, he shall be saved."—John x. 9.

F. A. B.   F. A. BLACKMER.

1. Oh, soul oppressed with sin and guilt, A Saviour's love and mercy see;
2. Oh, hear His words, accept the gift So free-ly offered now to thee;
3. His peace shall calm thy troubled mind, His love inspire thee when downcast;
4. The gracious in-vi-ta-tion heed; Let wisdom's choice be thine to-day;

To-day He calls in sweetest tones. And full sal-va-tion offers thee.
Throw off thy load so hard to bear: Let Christ thy burden-bearer be.
His presence cheer in eve-ry ill, His pow'r shall bring thee home at last.
The Saviour calls you to His fold; Oh, sin-ner, en-ter while you may.

CHORUS.

I am the door: by Me if any man enter in, He shall be saved, be saved;

By me if an-y man en-ter in, He shall be saved.

Going Home By and By.

No. 41.

F. A. B.

F. A. BLACKMER.

1. Christian, are you growing wea-ry? We are all go-ing home by and by;
2. Do the woes of life oppress thee? We are all go-ing home by and by;
3. Journey on a lit - tle long-er, We are all go-ing home by and by;
4. See! the light is growing clearer! We are all go-ing home by and by;
5. Soon we'll rest with Christ for-ev-er; We are all go-ing home by and by;

Does the way seem dark and dreary? We are all going home by and by.
And its tri - als sore dis-tress thee? We are all going home by and by.
With a faith a lit - tle stronger, We are all going home by and by.
And the heav'nly port is near-er; We are all going home by and by.
In a land where sin comes nev-er; We are all going home by and by.

CHORUS.

Go-ing home by and by, We are all go-ing
Go - ing home by and by,

home by and by, Go - ing home
by and by; Go - ing home

by and by, We are all go - ing home by and by.
by and by,

43

Thou Dear Redeemer.

No. 42.

A. F.

A. FRANCIS.

1. Thou dear Redeemer, dy - ing Lamb! We love to hear of Thee;
Thou dear Re - deemer, dying Lamb!

No music's like Thy charming name, Nor half so sweet to me, Nor half so sweet to me.
No mu - sic's like Thy charming name,

CHORUS.

We love to hear, Dear dy - ing Lamb, of Thee;
We love to hear, We love to hear of Thee;

No mu - sic's like Thy charming name, Nor half so sweet to me.

2. When we appear in yonder cloud,
With all the favor'd throng,
Then we will sing more sweet, more loud,
||: And Christ shall be our song :||

3. When we've been there ten thousand years,
Bright shining as the sun,

We've no less days to sing God's praise,
||: Than when we first begun. :||

4. Reach down, O Lord, thine arm of grace,
And cause me to attend
Where congregations ne'er break up,
||: And Sabbaths never end. :||

The Numberless Host.

No. 43.

"As the stars of the heaven, and as the sand which is upon the sea-shore." Gen. xxll. 17.

F. A. B.   F. A. BLACKMER.

1. When we en-ter the portals of glo - ry, And the great host of ransomed we see,
2. When we see all the saved of the a - ges Who from cruel death partings are free,
3. When we stand by the beautiful riv - er, 'Neath the shade of the life-giving tree,
4. When we look on the form that redeemed us, And his glory and majesty see,

As the numberless sand of the sea-shore, What a wonderful sight that will be.
Greeting there with a heavenly greeting, What a wonderful sight that will be.
Gazing out o'er the fair land of promise, What a wonderful sight that will be.
While as King of the saints he is reigning, What a wonderful sight that will be.

CHORUS.

of the sea - shore,

Num-ber-less as the sand   Num-ber-less as the sand,   Num-ber - less

of the shore,

as the sand, as the sand of the shore, Oh, what a sight 'twill be

When the ransomed host we see, As numberless as the sand of the sea - shore.

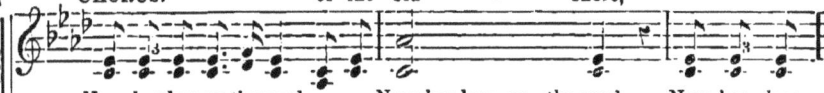

Golden Gates.

No. 44.

A. T. G.

A. T. GORHAM.
By permission.

1. O comrades, be not wea - ry, But brave-ly jour-ney on;...
2. Be - yond this vale of sor - row The morning land ap - pears
3. Then keep your spotless ban-ners Still wav-ing on be - fore.

Tho' dark the night and drear - y, Bright morn-ing soon will dawn;
Joy com - eth on the mor - row To ban - ish earth - ly fears;
Till vic - t'ry's loud ho - san - nas Resound from heaven's shore;

In yon-der star - lit man - sions, A crown of life a - waits
Press on, oh, wea - ry pil - grim, Where endless bliss a - waits
On, on! the goal is near - ing; Throw off all earth - ly weights,

The soul that keeps the prize in view, And enters the golden gates.
The faith-ful one that wins the crown, And enters the golden gates.
That you the heavenly prize may win, And enter the golden gates.

CHORUS.

Gold - en gates,.. Gold - en gates,..

O the beautiful, beautiful golden gates, O the beautiful, beautiful golden gates!

Golden Gates.—CONCLUDED.

With shout and song we journey a - long till we pass through the gold - en gates;

Gold - en gates,.. Gold - en gates,..

O the beautiful, beautiful golden gates, O the beautiful, beautiful golden gates!

There's vic - to - ry for you and me, When we en - ter the gol - den gates.

Abide With Me.

10s.

No. 45.

H. F. LYTE.

F. A. BLACKMER.

1. A - bide with me! Fast falls the eventide, The darkness deepens—Lord, with me abide.
2. Swift to its close ebbs out life's little day, Earth's joys grow dim, its glories pass away;
3. I need Thy presence every passing hour; What but Thy grace can foil the tempter's power?
4. I fear no foe, with Thee at hand to bless: Ills have no weight, and tears no bitterness;

When other helpers fail, and comforts flee, O Thou who changest not, abide with me!
Change and decay in all around I see; O Thou who changest not, abide with me!
Who, like Thyself, my Guide and Stay can be? Through cloud and sunshine, Lord, abide with me!
Where is death's sting? where, grave, thy victory? I triumph still if Thou abide with me.

47

What Manner of Man is This?

F. A. B.   F. A. BLACKMER.

1. "Save, Master, that we per- ish not," The poor dis - ci - ples loud besought;
2. Oh! this was Christ, the mighty Lord, Who stilled the tem- pest with a word;
3. Oh! seek this Christ, poor sinking soul, Round whom sin's billows threat'ning roll;

He spoke, and lo! the sea was calm; When they inquired, in great a - larm:
What heav'nly pow'r was there displayed! No wonder they, as- tonished, said:
His pow'r the tide of wrong shall stay, Till you, amazed, be- gin to say:

CHORUS.

"What man - ner of man is this? What man - ner of man is this,

What manner

That e- ven the winds and the sea o- bey Him? What man - ner of man is this?

What manner

What man - ner of man is this, That even the winds and the sea o- bey Him?"

48

It is Better Farther on.

No. 47.

F. A. BLACKMER.

Hark! a voice from E - den steal - ing, Such as but to an - gels known, Hope its song of cheer is sing - ing, "It is bet - ter far - ther on."

CHORUS.

It is bet - ter farther on, It is bet - ter farther on, It is bet - ter farther on, It is bet - ter farther on.

2 Hope is singing, still is singing,
Softly in an under tone;
Singing as if God had taught it,
"It is better farther on."
Cho.

3 Night and day it sings the same song,
Sings it when I sit alone;
Sings it so the heart may hear it,
"It is better farther on."
Cho.

4 On the grave it sits and sings it,
Sings it when the heart would groan;
Sings it when the shadows darken,
"It is better farther on."
Cho.

5 Farther on! Oh! how much farther?
Count the mile-stones one by one;
No! no counting, only trusting,
"It is better farther on."
Cho.

Peace! Be Still!

"Jesus rebuked the wind, and said unto the sea, Peace! be still!" Mark 4: 39.

MISS M. A. BAKER.

H. R. PALMER.
By permission.

1. Master, the tempest is rag - ing! The billows are tossing high!
2. Master, with anguish of spir - it I bow in my grief to - day;
3. Master, the ter - ror is o - ver, The el - e-ments sweetly rest;

The sky is o'ershadowed with blackness, No shelter or help is nigh;
The depths of my sad heart are troub-led; Oh, waken and save, I pray!
Earth's sun in the calm lake is mirrored, And heaven's within my breast;

"Car - est Thou not that we per - ish?"— How canst Thou lie a - sleep,
Torrents of sin and of an - guish Sweep o'er my sink-ing soul;
Lin - ger, O bless-ed Re - deem - er; Leave me a-lone no more;

When each moment so madly is threat'ning A grave in the angry deep?
And I per-ish! I perish! dear Master; Oh has-ten, and take con-trol.
And with joy I shall make the blest harbor, And rest on the blissful shore.

CHORUS.

"The winds and the waves shall obey my will, Peace! be still!....

Peace! be still! peace! be still!

Whether the wrath of the storm-tossed sea, Or demons, or men, or what -

ev - er it be, No water can swal-low the ship where lies The

Master of ocean, and earth, and skies; They all shall sweetly o - bey My will,

Peace! be still! Peace! be still! They all shall sweetly obey My will; Peace! peace! be still!

Daybreak.

No. 49.

ANNIE HERBERT.   F. A. BLACKMER.

1. When the clouds have left the hill - tops, And the beau - ty of the day
2. When the darkness rolls from o - cean, And the light beams brightly o'er
3. When the pain and wasting fe - ver, And the thou-sand ills of life,
4. When the graves of earth are o-pened, And the fair, lov'd forms arise,
5. When the Ci - ty, grand, e - ter - nal, Shall descend 'mid clouds of light,

Gleams a - long thro' gold - en por - tals, Melting all the mists a-way,
Eve - ry wave and foam - ing bil - low, Dashing 'gainst this mortal shore,
All are healed by one Phy-si - cian, And for-ev-er hushed the strife,
Springing up from dust - y cham - bers, Soaring upward to the skies,
And the King bids saints to en - ter Mansions filled with ho-ly light,

Then no more will shadows dark - en, Till the way we can-not see—
Then the heart will sing with rap-ture, And the voice break forth in praise
Then sweet peace and ho - ly com - fort Will pos-sess the inmost soul,
Then sweet waves of thrill-ing mu - sic Will entrance the listening ear,
Then the life-work of all a - ges Will receive a just reward,

Oh, for Thee our hearts are yearning, Glory of e-ter - ni - ty.
To the God that rules the tempest: "Just and true are all Thy ways."
For the wea - ry, homesick pilgrim Will have reached the long'd-for goal.
"Like the sound of man-y waters," Murmuring gent - ly, soft and clear.
Home with Je - sus, sweet rest giv - en, In the king-dom of our Lord.

52

Daybreak. CONCLUDED.

Oh, for Thee our hearts are yearning, Glo - ry of   e - ter - ni - ty.
To the   God that rules the temp - est: "Just and true are all Thy ways."
For the   wea - ry, homesick pilgrim Will have reached the long'd-for goal.
"Like the sound of man-y   wa - ters," Murmuring gent-ly, soft and clear.
Home with Je-sus, sweet rest giv - en,   In the   king - dom of our Lord.

CHORUS.

Oh, the joy, ... that day shall bring, ...   Oh, the   songs   we then shall
Oh, the joy   that day shall bring,   Oh, the songs

sing, ... When the   clouds ...   of earth have lift - ed, And the
we then shall sing,   When the clouds

mists. ..... have cleared away;   When the clouds of earth have
And the mists   have cleared away;

a - way.
lift - ed, And the   mists have cleared. have   cleared a - way.

53

We Shall See.

I. I. LESLIE.

F. A. BLACKMER.

1. When the skies shall glow and brighten With the beams of endless day,
2. When no more with clouded vis - ion Gaze we toward that far-off land,
3. When this weary watch is o - ver, And for rest no more we sigh,

And the dark and dreary shad-ows From our vis - ion flee a - way,
And in faith and hope grow weary, Waiting for the an - gel band,
When the friends we love are near us, And no more we see them die,

We shall see what now is hid - den; On that fair un - fad - ing shore,
We shall see where they shall gather— All the ransomed and the free;
We shall see those promised mansions Towering by the crys - tal sea,

We shall walk and sing for - ev - er, And be wea - ry nev - er - more.
We shall meet and know each other, And for - ev - er blest shall be.
And the glori - ous, hea - venly city Shin - ing on e - ter - nal - ly.

CHORUS.

We shall see as we are seen, with no clouds to intervene,
We shall see as we are seen, with no clouds to intervene.

54

In the com - ing of the morning, When the shad - ows flee away, flee away;
In the coming   When the shadows

shad - ows

In the com - ing of the morning, When the shadows, when the shadows flee away.
In the coming

shad - ows

Wanderer, Come.

No. 51.

"While it is called to-day."

A. F.

A. FRANCIS.

1. Wanderer, come to Je - sus, Come without de - lay; Seek His lov - ing
2. Wanderer, come to Je - sus, Come, O come to - day; Leave the path of
3. Wanderer, come to Je - sus, Heed the warning voice; Now, while mercy

REFRAIN.

fa - vor, Nev - ermore to stray. Come, O come: come, O come
er - ror, For the heav'nly way.
lin-gers, Come and make the choice.

while 'tis called today; Come, O come; come, O come, Come while yet you may!

55

Is Your Lamp Burning?

No. 52.

"Let your light so shine before men, that they may see your good works,
and glorify your Father which is in heaven."

Words arranged by F. A. B.

F. A. BLACKMER.

1. Say, is your lamp burning, my brother? I pray you look quickly and see,
2. There are many and many around you, Who follow where-ever you go;
3. If once all the lamps that are lighted Should stead-i-ly blaze in a line,
4. We hear that the Bridegroom is coming, To meet Him with lamps we must go;

For if it were burning, then surely Some beams would fall brightly on me.
If you tho't that they walked in the shadow, Your lamp would burn brighter, I know:
Then wide o'er the land and the o-cean, The light of the gospel would shine;
And oil we must take in our ves-sels, That every flame brightly may glow;

Straight, straight is the road, but I fal-ter, And yet may fall out by the way;
And some on dark mountains have stumbled, Have fall-en on rocks, where they lie,
And many who now grope in darkness, And man-y now go-ing a-stray,
Then trim your lamp brighter, my brother, And suffer it not to grow dim,

Then lift your lamp higher, my brother, Lest I should make fatal de-lay.
With their white, pleading faces turned upward To the clouds and the pitiful sky.
By the wonderful light would, most surely, Be guid-ed back in-to the way.
That when He shall come to the marriage, You glad-ly may en-ter with Him.

CHORUS.

Oh, is........ your lamp burn - ing? I pray you look quickly and see.
Oh, is your lamp burning? Oh, is your lamp burning?

Is Your Lamp Burning?—CONCLUDED.

For if it were burning, most surely   Some beams would fall brightly on me.

Since I've Learned to Trust Him More.

No. 53.

F. A. B.   F. A. BLACKMER.

1. Once I tho't I walked with Jesus,   Yet such changeful feelings had;
2. But He called me clos-er   to Him, Bade my doubting, fearing,   cease;
3. Now I'm trusting ev-'ry   moment, Nothing less can be e - nough;

Sometimes trusting, sometimes doubting, Sometimes joyful, sometimes sad.
And when I had ful-ly   yield-ed, Filled my soul with per-fect   peace.
And the Saviour bears me gently   O'er those places once so   rough.

CHORUS.

Oh, the peace the Saviour gives, Peace I nev-er know be - fore;

And my way has brighter grown, Since I've learned to trust Him more.

Home, Crown and Song.

No. 54.

A. T. G.

A. T. GORHAM.
By permission.

DEUTT.

1. Beautiful home, beautiful home, Beautiful home where weary ones rest;
2. Beautiful crowns, beautiful crowns, Beautiful crowns the glo-ri-fied wear;
3. Beautiful song, beautiful song, Song of the blest on heaven's bright shore;

Beau-ti-ful home, beautiful home, Beautiful home, home of the blest.
Beau-ti-ful crowns, beautiful crowns, Sparkling on brows heavenly fair,
Beau-ti-ful song, beautiful song, Beautiful song heard ev-er-more.

Beautiful home where God is the light; Beautiful home of an-gels bright;
Beautiful crowns of gems and gold, Gift of a Saviour's love un-told;
Song of the countless seraphs that stand Striking their harps at God's right hand;

Home where the blood-washed walk in white, We long, oh, we long to be there.
Beau-ti-ful crowns laid up of old— We long, oh, we long to be there.
Bless-ed, thrice blessed an-gel band! We long, oh, we long to be there.

CHORUS.

Beautiful home,...... Beau-ti-ful home,...... Beautiful home.
Beau-ti-ful home, Beau-ti-ful home, Beautiful, beau-ti-ful

58

Home, Crown and Song.—Concluded.

where wea-ry ones rest;........ Beau-ti-ful home!......
home where the wea-ry ones,wea-ry ones rest;

Beau-ti-ful home!

Beau-ti-ful home!...... Beautiful, beautiful home of the blest,of the blest.
Beau-ti-ful home!

In the Silent Midnight Watches.

No. 55.

REV. A. C. COXE.   F. A. BLACKMER.

1. In the silent mid-night watches,List—thy oosom's door!How it knocketh,knocketh,
2. Death comes down with ruthless footsteps,To the hall and hut; Think you death will tar-ry
3. Then 'tis time to stand en-treating Christ to let thee in: At the gate of heav-en

knocketh,knocketh ever more! Say not 'tis thy pulses beating,'Tis thy heart of sin;
knocking When the door is shut? Jesus waiteth,waiteth,waiteth;But the door is fast;
beating, Wailing for thy sin! Nay! alas,thou guilty creature! Hast thou,then,forgot?

'Tis the Saviour knocks,and crieth,"Rise,and let me in! Rise, and let me in!"
Grieved, away thy Saviour go-eth,Death breaks in at last. Death breaks in at last.
Je-sus waited long to know thee;Now He knows thee not.Now He knows thee not.

59

O, To Be Ready.

No. 56.

O. R. B.   O. R. BARROWS.

1. O, to be ready, ready, Ready my Lord to meet;
2. O, to be ready, ready, Ready as man can be,
3. O, to be ready, ready, Ready to join the song;

List'ning to hear his foot-fall, Watching His smile to greet;
Do-ing with joy each du-ty, Suf-fer-ing pa-tient-ly;
Swelling the an-gel cho-rus, Shouting a-mid the throng;

Trimming my lamp that my neighbor May not in darkness be found;
Speaking a word in its sea-son, Scatt'ring the life-giving bread;
Hear-ing Thy welcome with gladness, Showing Thee gems for the crown,

Wielding the sword of the Spirit, Guarding Imman-uel's ground.
Spreading a-broad in the des-ert Streams from the Fountain-head.
Plucked as the brand from the burning, Won 'mid the scoff and frown.

CHORUS.

O, to be ready, O, to be ready. Read-y when Je-sus shall

60

come; Bearing my sheaves from the harvest, Guiding poor wand'rers home.

After.

No. 57.

I. I. LESLIE.

F. A. BLACKMER.

1. Af-ter the storm that sweeps the sea; Af-ter the drift - ing to the lea;
2. Af-ter the win - ter long and drear; Af-ter the snow-clouds dis - ap - pear;
3. Af-ter the long and toilsome day; Af-ter the sun's fierce, burning ray;
4. Af-ter the course of life is run; Af-ter its work has all been done;
5. Af-ter the march of time shall cease; Af-ter earth-strife shall end in peace:

Af-ter the rocks and sands are passed, Cometh the joy of home at last.
Af-ter the winds sweet o - dors bring, Cometh the ev - er welcome spring.
Af-ter the toil - er homeward goes, Cometh the night and sweet re - pose.
Af-ter the hands are on the breast, Cometh the long and peaceful rest.
Af-ter the changeful dis - ap-pears, Cometh the long, e - ter - nal years.

REFRAIN.

Af - ter all that here we see, What will there be, what will there be?

Af - ter all that here we see, Af-ter all, e - ter - ni - ty.

Behold, What Love!

F. A. B.

F. A. BLACKMER.

1. Be-hold, what love! what boundless love, The Fa-ther hath be - stow'd
2. Tho' now indeed the sons of God, The world knoweth us not;
3. What we shall soon in glo - ry be, It doth not yet ap - pear;
4. And ev - 'ry man that hath this hope, Himself doth pu - ri - fy,

Up - on His ser - vants that they should Be call'd the sons of God.
Be - cause it knew not Christ, the Lord, Who hath our son-ship bought.
But this we know, that when He comes, We shall His im-age bear.
E - ven as He, our Lord, is pure, In whom no sin doth lie.

Up - on His ser - vants that they should Be call'd the sons of God.
Because it knew not Christ, the Lord, Who hath our son-ship bought.
But this we know, that when He comes, We shall His im-age bear.
E - ven as He, our Lord, is pure, In whom no sin doth lie.

CHORUS.

Be - hold, what manner of love!.............. Be - hold, what manner of
Behold, what manner of love, what manner of love! Behold, what manner of

love!.............. Be - hold, what manner of love!..............
love, what manner of love! Behold, what manner of love, what manner of love!

Behold, What Love!—CONCLUDED.

The Fa-ther hath bestow'd up - on us, That we
We should be

should be call'd, Be call'd the sons of God.
call'd the sons of God,

My Crucified Lord.

No. 59.

A. F.

A. FRANCIS.

1. Now will I praise Thy name, And sing Thy wondrous fame;
2. For me Thy blood was spilt; Thou didst re - move my guilt;
3. Tho' men may mock and sneer, For Thee I'll suf - fer here,
4. When Thou shalt come a - gain I shall be freed from pain,
5. Till then for this I pine To see Thy face Di - vine,

Thou, who for sin - ners came, My cru - ci - fied Lord.
And save, I know Thou wilt, My cru - ci - fied Lord.
For Thou wilt soon ap - pear, My cru - ci - fied Lord.
And in Thy king - dom reign, My cru - ci - fied Lord.
And in Thine im - age shine, My cru - ci - fied Lord.

63

The Child of a King.

No. 60.

HATTIE E. BUEL.

REV. JOHN B. SUMNER.

1. My Father is rich in hou-ses and lands, He holdeth the wealth of the
2. My Father's own Son, the Saviour of men, Once wandered o'er earth as the
3. I once was an outcast-stranger on earth, A sin-ner by choice, and an
4. A tent or a cot-tage, why should I care? They're building a palace for

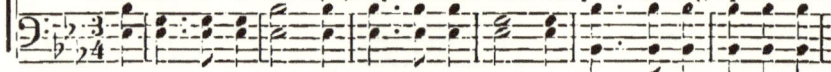

world in His hands! Of rubies and diamonds, of sil-ver and gold, His
poor-est of them; But now He is reigning in glo-ry on high, And will
al-ien by birth! But I've been adopted, my name's written down,—An
me o-ver there! Tho' ex-iled from home, yet, still I may sing: All

CHORUS.

coffers are full,—He has riches un-told.
give me a home when He comes by and by.
heir to a mansion, a robe, and a crown.
glo-ry to God, I'm the child of a King.
I'm the child of a King, The

child of a King; With Je-sus my Saviour, I'm the child of a King.

As arr. in "Songs of the New Life," by per. John J. Hood.

Simply Trusting Christ My Lord.

No. 61.

F. A. B.

F. A. BLACKMER.

1. Simp-ly trust-ing Christ my Lord, Simp-ly trust-ing ev'-ry day;
2. Trusting when the shades of night Hide each glim'ring, guid-ing ray;
3. Trusting when the heart is light, Trusting 'neath a load of care;
4. Simp-ly trust-ing, ev-en when Ev'-ry cher-ished hope is gone,
5. Simp-ly trust-ing to the end Of this earth-ly pil-grim way,

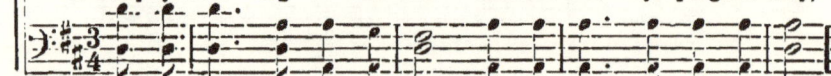

64

Simply Trusting Christ my Lord.—CONCLUDED.

Trusting Him whate'er be-tide, As I walk the nar-row way.
Trusting Him I yet can sing, As I on-ward press my way.
On the moun-tain, in the vale, Trusting Je - sus ev'rywhere.
And each earth-ly prop removed, That my poor heart leaned upon.
When my faith shall end in sight, And my night in per-fect day.

CHORUS.

Simp-ly trust-ing, simply trusting, Trust-ing Je-sus day by day;

Thro' life's long and toilsome journey, Simply trusting all the way.

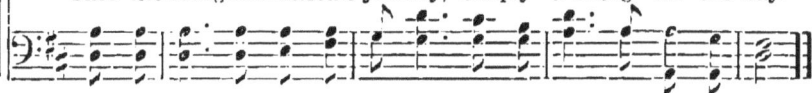

Frederick.

F. A. B.

No. 62.

1. Softly now the light of day Fades up-on our sight away; Free from care, from labor free,
2. Soon for us the light of day Shall for-ev-er pass away; Then, from sin and sorrow free,

Lord, we would commune with Thee; Free from care, from labor free, We would commune with Thee.
Take us, Lord, to dwell with Thee; Then, from sin and sorrow free, Take us to dwell with Thee.

65

Go Tell the Gospel Story.

No. 63.

LUCY D. HARRINGTON.   F. A. BLACKMER.

1. Go tell the gos-pel sto - ry, Of love so pure and free;
2. Go tell the gos-pel sto - ry, Of love so pure and free;
3. Go tell the gos-pel sto - ry, And warn of com-ing woe;

Tell of a bless - ed Sav - iour Who died for you and me;
Tell of the com - ing glo - ry, When we with Christ shall be.
Win man - y souls to Je - sus, That they His love may know.

Go tell how much He suf-fered Up - on the cru - el tree.
Go tell the joy - ful sto - ry, Proclaim it far and near.
Go tell the wondrous sto - ry, Re-peat it o'er and o'er,

That all might have sal - va - tion, And live e - ter - nal - ly.
That man - y now in dark - ness The bless - ed news may hear.
And wea - ry not with tell - ing, Till time shall be no more.

CHORUS.

Go tell the gos-pel sto - ry, Of love so pure and free;

66

Tell of the bless-ed Sav-iour Who died for you and me.

Together They are Growing.

"Let both grow together until the harvest; and in the time of harvest I will say to the reapers, Gather ye together first the tares, and bind them in bundles to burn them: but gather the wheat into my barn.
* * * The harvest is the end of the world; and the reapers are the angels."—Matt. xiii: 30. 39.

No. 64.

A. F.   A. FRANCIS.

1. To - geth - er they are grow - ing, The wheat be-side the tares;
2. E'en now the fields are whit - ened, And read - y do ap - pear
3. Let us improve each mo - ment, In love and works a - bound;

The sun-shine of God's mer - cy For har - vest each pre - pares.
For work of an - gel reap - ers,—The har - vest must be near.
That we may in the har - vest A-mong the wheat be found.

Chorus.

They are ripening, ripening, Ripening for the har - vest;

The wheat for the garner, The tares for the burning, The reapers soon will come.

The Angel Keepers.

"That great city, the holy Jerusalem........ ... having the glory of God.......... and had a wall great and high, and had twelve gates, and at the gates twelve angels.......... and the twelve gates were twelve pearls; every several gate was of one pearl."—Rev. xxi: 10, 11, 12, 21.

No. 65.

LUCY D. HARRINGTON.

F. A. BLACKMER.

1. By faith we view our promised home, And see the ci - ty's glorious light;
2. Oh, home, sweet home, for thee we yearn, Where we shall be with an - gel peers,
3. Oh, home, sweet home, for thee we wait; Our Father's house, with mansions rare;

Its pearl - y gates and streets of gold, Where faith shall end in per - fect sight.
Where we shall walk with Christ in white, And God shall wipe away all tears,
We long to pass thy pearly gates, And dwell with God and an-gels there;

An an - gel guards each gate of pearl, Twelve an - gel keepers bright and fair;
We long to walk the golden streets And gath - er by the riv - er's side,
Our Bridegroom-King, we wait for thee; Oh, haste and bring the perfect day!

None but the pure can en - ter in, None but the saved find welcome there.
To eat the fruit of life's fair tree, Where sin and death no more di - vide.
Come, quick-ly come, and take us home; Thy kingdom come, oh Lord, we pray.

CHORUS.

Can you pass the keepers at the gates, The an - gel keepers bright and fair?

68

The Angel Keepers.—CONCLUDED.

Can you en-ter thro' the gates of pearl? Can you pass the ho - ly an - gels there?

The Blood Alone.

No. 66.

F. A. B.

F. A. BLACKMER.

1. There is no work that I can do And thus for sin a - tone;
2. There is no way sought out by man That stands for sin a cure;
3. The fount be-hold, sin-burdened one, And to it quick-ly flee,

The pre - cious blood of Je-sus Christ Must save, and that a - lone.
Nought but the pre - cious blood applied Can make the cleansing sure.
And plunge beneath the crimson flood, And rise from sin made free.

CHORUS.

The blood, the blood, the precious blood! The blood of Christ a - lone

Can all the load of guilt remove, And change the heart of stone.

69

We Shall Not All Sleep.

F. A. B.

"We shall not all sleep, but we shall all be changed."

F. A. BLACKMER.

1. We shall not all sleep the Bi-ble declares, Low in the grave ere the Lord shall appear;
2. We shall not all sleep but we shall be changed, When Jesus comes and our waiting is o'er;
4. Oh,'twill be grand all His works to behold, When with His angels the Lord shall descend;

Some will be liv-ing and watching for Him, Marking the signs which denote He is near.
Changed in a moment and made like our Lord, Glorious, immortal, to die nev-er-more.
Changing the liv-ing and raising the dead, Making of sorrow and earth-strife an end.

CHORUS.

There will be some who will not taste death, Some who will say when the Lord shall come,

"This is our God, we have waited for Him, And He will save us and take us home."

There's Resting By-and-by.

"There remaineth a rest therefore to the people of God."

F. A. BLACKMER.

1. When faint and weary, toiling, With sweat-drops on my brow, I long to rest from
2. Nor say, when over-burdened, You ask for friendly aid, "Why i - dle stands my
3. Wan reap-er in the harvest, Let this thy strength sustain; Each sheaf that fills the

la - bor,   To drop the burden now, There comes a gentle chiding,   To quell each
bro:h-er,   No yoke up-on him laid?"   The Master bids him tar - ry, And dare you
gar-ner;   Brings you e - ter-nal gain;   Then bear the cross with patience, To fields of

mourn-ing sigh; Work while the day is   shin-ing, There's resting by - and - by.
ask Him why? Go, la - bor in His vineyard, There's resting by - and - by.
du - ty hie: 'Tis sweet to work for   Je - sus, There's resting by - and - by

CHORUS.

There's rest-ing by - and - by, There's resting by - and - by, We shall not al-ways

la-bor, We shall not always cry; The end is drawing near-er, The end for

which we sigh; We'll lay our heavy   bur - dens down, There's resting by-and-by.

71

INDEX.

Titles in Small Caps. First Lines in Romans.

www.ingramcontent.com/pod-product-compliance
Lightning Source LLC
Chambersburg PA
CBHW020240090426
42735CB00010B/1770